MW01067674

CONTENTS

10-NOTE KALIMBA IN C SCALE

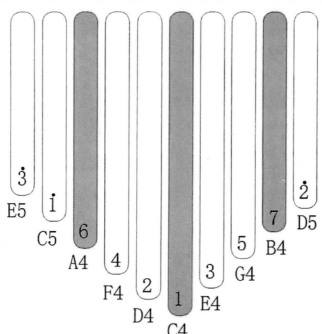

17-NOTE KALIMBA IN C SCALE

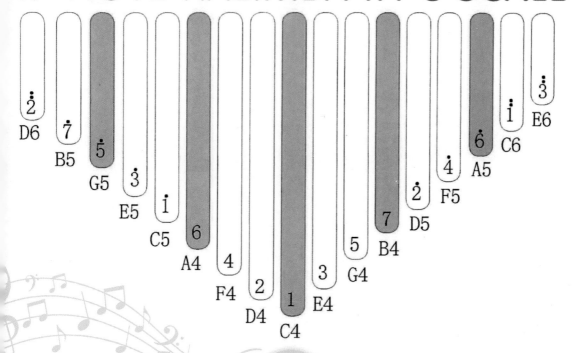

TUNING

If you want good sound, you must tune the keys. You can either use an entity tuner, or you can download a tuner app from your mobile phone. Android System app: gstrings, ISO System app: Instuner.

Note: Sometimes the tuner is not sensitive to the keys in the high-pitched position. There may be resonance when you first start playing. Press the keys nearby softly, and then tune your kalimba.

BUZZING SOUND

If the keys make a slight buzzing noise, this happens occasionally. Simply move the keys left and right softly. If this doesn't work, just place a paper card between the key and the bridge to solve the problem.

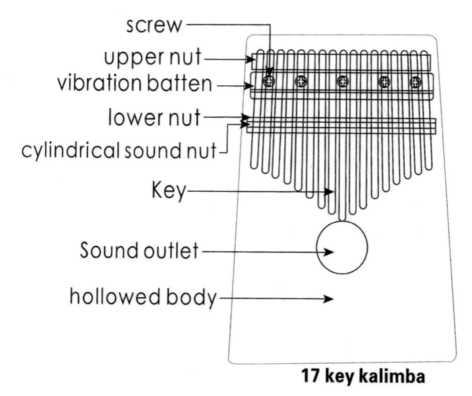

screw
upper nut
vibration batten
lower nut
cylindrical sound nut
Key
Sound outlet
hollowed body

17 key kalimba

CARE FOR YOUR KALIMBA

When not playing the kalimba, please store it in the bag. Please keep your kalimba at a relative humidity level of between 30 to 60 percent. If the products gets damp, rust can cause problems with the resonance of the keys.

HOW TO HOLD AND PLAY YOUR KALIMBA

- Hold the kalimba with your your thumb at the keys and your other fingers on the side.
- Using your nails to strike the kesy will minimize finger pain and make the sound more crisp.
- Use your middle finger to cover the hole on the back to create a WAH sound.
- Train your thumb to move easily between all the keys on each side.

NOTES AND STICKERS

For some melodies, we group circles to show rhythm.

Places the attached stickers with notes on the kalimba keys. They will help you begin to play immediately, even you have never played before.

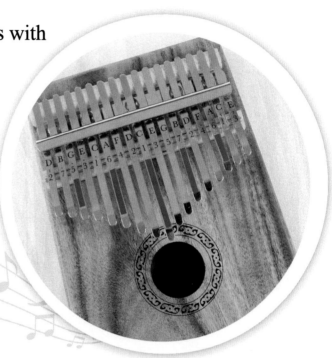

Usually the kalimba is considered an adult instrument, but with our visual, your kids will easily begin to play as well. These stickers have both letter notes and numbers. You can find a lot of sheet music for the kalimba online, but only with numbers which correspond to your kalimba.

KtabS is a music notation system which was written especially for the kalimba. You can find this in most places and this notation can easily be read. However, we suggest that the easiest way to begin is to play with the letter notes in our book.

Hot Cross Buns

(E) (D) (C)

Hot Cross Buns,

(E) (D) (C)

Hot Cross Buns,

(C) (C) (C) (C)

One a pen - ny,

(D) (D) (D) (D)

two a pen - ny,

(E) (D) (C)

Hot Cross Buns

Are you sleeping?

(C) (D) (E) (C) (C) (D) (E) (C)
Are you sleeping, are you sleeping?

(E) (F) (G) (E) (F) (G)
Brother John, Brother John?

(G) (A) (G) (F) (E) (C)
Morning bells are ringing,

(G) (A) (G) (F) (E) (C)
morning bells are ringing

(D) (G) (C) (D) (G) (C)
Ding ding dong, ding ding dong.

For a more voiced sound, change the keys and play this variation

(G) (A) (B) (G) (G) (A) (B) (G)
Are you sleeping, are you sleeping?

(B) (C) (D) (B) (C) (D)
Brother John, Brother John?

(D) (E) (D) (C) (B) (G)
Morning bells are ringing,

(D) (E) (D) (C) (B) (G)
morning bells are ringing

(A) (D) (G) (A) (D) (G)
Ding ding dong, ding ding dong.

Mary Had A Little Lamb

(E) (D) (C) (D) (E) (E) (E)

Mary had a little lamb

(D) (D) (D) (E) (G) (G)

Little lamb, little lamb

(E) (D) (C) (D) (E) (E) (E)

Mary had a little lamb

(E) (D) (D) (E) (D) (C)

Its fleece was white as snow

The Wheels On The Bus

(C) (F) (F) (F) (F) (A) (Ç) (A) (F)

The wheels on the bus go round and round.

(G) (E) (C) (Ç) (A) (F)

Round and round. Round and round.

(C) (F) (F) (F) (F) (A) (Ç) (A) (F)

The wheels on the bus go round and round.

(G) (C) (C) (F)

Round and round.

SCHOOL BUS

9

Twinkle, Twinkle Little Star

Ⓒ   Ⓒ   Ⓖ   Ⓖ   Ⓐ   Ⓐ   Ⓖ

Twin-kle, twin-kle, lit-tle star

Ⓕ   Ⓕ   Ⓔ   Ⓔ   Ⓓ   Ⓓ   Ⓒ

How I won-der what you are.

Ⓖ Ⓖ Ⓕ   Ⓕ   Ⓔ   Ⓔ Ⓓ

Up a-bove the world so high,

Ⓖ   Ⓖ   Ⓕ   Ⓕ   Ⓔ   Ⓔ   Ⓓ

Like a dia-mond in the sky.

Old MacDonald Had A Farm

(G) (G) (G) (D) (E) (E) (D) (B)(B)(A)(A)(G)

Old McDonald had a farm. E-I-E-I-O.

(D) (G) (G) (G) (D) (E) (E) (D)

And on that farm he had a cow.

(B)(B)(A)(A)(G)

E-I-E-I-O.

(D) (D) (G) (G) (G)

With a moo moo here.

(D) (D) (G) (G) (G)

With a moo moo here.

(G) (G) (G)

Here a moo.

(G) (G) (G)

There a moo.

(G) (G) (G) (G) (G) (G)

Everywhere a moo moo.

(G) (G) (G)(D) (E)(E)(D) (B)(B)(A)(A)(G)

Old McDonald had a farm. E-I-E-I-O.

Do You Know The Muffin Man?

(C) (C) (F) (F) (G) (A) (F) (F)

Oh, do you know the muf-fin man

(E) (D) (G) (G) (F) (E) (C) (C)

The muf-fin man, the muf-fin man

(C) (C) (F) (F) (G) (A) (F) (F)

Oh, do you know the muf-fin man

(F) (G) (G) (C) (C) (F)

That lives on Dru-ry Lane?

London Bridge is Falling Down

G   A G F E F G

London Bridge is falling down,

D E F   E F G

Falling down, falling down.

G   A G F E F G

London Bridge is falling down,

D G E C

My fair lady.

Jingle bells

(E) (E) (E) (E) (E) (E)
Jingle bells, jingle bells,
(E) (G) (C) (D) (E)
jingle all the way
(F) (F) (F) (F) (F) (E) (E)
Oh, what fun it is to ride
(E) (E) (D) (D) (E) (D) (G)
in a one horse open sleigh
(E) (E) (E) (E) (E) (E)
Jingle bells, jingle bells,
(E) (G) (C) (D) (E)
jingle all the way
(F) (F) (F) (F) (F) (E) (E)
Oh, what fun it is to ride
(E) (G) (G) (F) (D) (C)
in a one horse open sleigh

For a more voiced sound,
change the keys and play
this variation

(E) (E) (E) (E) (E) (E)
Jingle bells, jingle bells,
(E) (G) (C) (D) (E)
jingle all the way
(F) (F) (F) (F) (F) (E) (E)
Oh, what fun it is to ride
(E) (D) (D) (C) (D) (G)
in a one horse open sleigh
(E) (E) (E) (E) (E) (E)
Jingle bells, jingle bells,
(E) (G) (C) (D) (E)
jingle all the way
(F) (F) (F) (F) (F) (E) (E)
Oh, what fun it is to ride
(E) (G) (G) (F) (D) (C)
in a one horse open sleigh

We wish you a Merry Christmas

Ⓒ Ⓕ Ⓕ Ⓖ Ⓕ Ⓔ Ⓓ Ⓓ

We wish you a Mer-ry Christ-mas

Ⓓ Ⓖ Ⓖ Ⓐ Ⓖ Ⓕ Ⓔ Ⓒ

We wish you a Mer-ry Christ-mas

Ⓒ Ⓐ Ⓐ Ⓐ Ⓐ Ⓖ Ⓕ Ⓓ

We wish you a Mer-ry Christ-mas

Ⓒ Ⓒ Ⓓ Ⓖ Ⓔ Ⓕ

And a Hap-py New Year

15

Brahms' Lullaby
(Lullaby and Goodnight)

Ⓔ Ⓔ Ⓖ Ⓔ Ⓔ Ⓖ
Lullaby, and good night,

Ⓔ Ⓖ Ⓒ̣ Ⓑ Ⓐ Ⓐ Ⓖ
With pink roses bedight,

Ⓓ Ⓔ Ⓕ Ⓓ Ⓓ Ⓔ Ⓕ
With lilies o'er spread,

Ⓓ Ⓕ Ⓑ Ⓐ Ⓖ Ⓑ Ⓒ̣
Is my baby's sweet head.

Ⓒ Ⓒ Ⓒ̣ Ⓐ Ⓕ Ⓖ
Lay you down now, and rest,

Ⓔ Ⓒ Ⓕ Ⓖ Ⓐ Ⓖ
May your slumber be blessed!

Ⓒ Ⓒ Ⓒ̣ Ⓐ Ⓕ Ⓖ
Lay you down now, and rest,

Ⓔ Ⓒ Ⓕ Ⓔ Ⓓ Ⓒ
May your slumber be blessed!

16

Ode to Joy

E E F G G F E D

C C D E E D D

E E F G G F E D

C C D E D C C

D D E C D E F E C

D E F E D C D G

E E F G G F E D

C C D E D C C

Happy Birthday

(C) (C) (D) (C) (F) (E)

Happy birthday to you

(C) (C) (D) (C) (G) (F)

Happy birthday to you

(C) (C) (Ç) (A) (F) (F) (E) (D)

Happy birthday dear Mary

(Ç) (Ç) (A) (F) (G) (F)

Happy birthday to you

18

Le Cucaracha

Oh! Susannah

C D E G G A G E
Oh! I come from A-la-ba-ma

C D E E D C D
With my ban-jo on my knee

C D E G G A G E
I'm going to Louis-i-a-na

C D E E D D C
My true love for to see.

F F A A
Oh! Su-san-nah,

G   G E C D
Don't you cry for me

C D E G G A G E
I come from A-la-ba-ma

C D E E D D C
With my Ban-jo on my knee

Itsy Bitsy Spider

Ⓒ Ⓒ Ⓒ Ⓒ Ⓓ Ⓔ Ⓔ

The itsy-bitsy spider

Ⓔ Ⓓ Ⓒ Ⓓ Ⓔ Ⓒ

Climbed up the water spout

Ⓔ Ⓔ Ⓕ Ⓖ

Down came the rain

Ⓖ Ⓕ Ⓔ Ⓕ Ⓖ Ⓔ

And washed the spider out

Ⓒ Ⓒ Ⓓ Ⓔ

Out came the sun

Ⓔ Ⓓ Ⓒ Ⓓ Ⓔ Ⓒ

And dried up all the rain

Ⓒ Ⓒ Ⓒ Ⓒ Ⓓ Ⓔ Ⓔ

And the itsy-bitsy spider

Ⓔ Ⓓ Ⓒ Ⓓ Ⓔ Ⓒ

Climbed up the spout again

The First Noel

(E) (D) (C)　(D) (E) (F) (G)
The　Fir -　st　No -　　el,

(A) (B) (Ç)　(B) (A) (G)
The　An -　gels did　say

(A) (B) (Ç)　(B) (A) (G) (A) (B) (Ç)　(G) (F) (E)
Was to　cer -　tain poorshep herds　in　fields where they lay

(E) (D) (C)　(D) (E) (F) (G)
In　fie -　lds　whe - re　they

(A) (B) (Ç)　(B) (A) (G)
Lay　keep -　ing their sheep

(A) (B) (Ç)　(B) (A) (G) (A) (B) (Ç)　(G) (F) (E)
On　a　cold　win - ter's ni - ght that　was　　so　deep

(E) (D) (C)　(D) (E) (F) (G)　(Ç) (B) (A) (A) (G)
No -　el,　　No -　el,　　No -　el,　　No - e

(Ç) (B) (A) (G) (A) (B) (Ç)　(G) (F) (E)
Born　is　the　Ki - ng　of　Is -　　ra - el!

Yankee Doodle

C C D E C E D
Yankee Doodle went to town

C C D E C B
riding on a pony,

C C D E F E D
Stuck a feather in his cap

C B G A B Ç Ç
And called it macaroni.

A B A G A B Ç
Yankee Doodle keep it up,

G A G F E G
Yankee Doodle dandy,

A B A G A B Ç
Mind the music and the step,

A G Ç B Ḍ Ç Ç
And with the girls be handy.

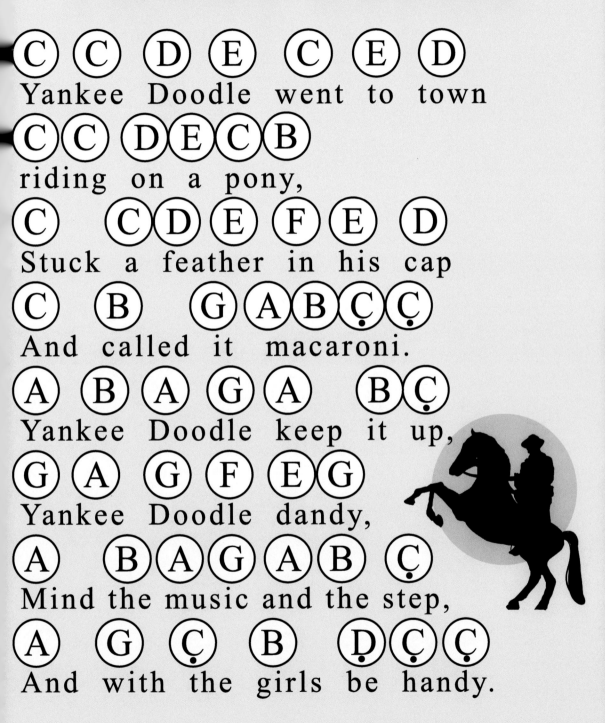

23

Row, row, row your boat

(C)   (C)   (C)   (D)   (E)

Row, row, row your boat,

(E)   (D) (E)   (F)   (G)

Gently down the stream.

(C)(C)(C)(G)(G)(G)(E)(E)(E)(C)(C)(C)

Merrily, merrily, merrily, merrily,

(G)   (F)(E)(D)(C)

Life is but a dream.

24

Jolly Old Saint Nicholas

Ⓐ Ⓐ Ⓐ Ⓐ Ⓖ Ⓖ Ⓖ
Jolly old Saint Nicholas,

Ⓕ Ⓕ Ⓕ Ⓕ Ⓐ
Lean your ear this way.

Ⓓ Ⓓ Ⓓ ⒹⒸⒸ Ⓕ
Don't you tell a single soul

Ⓖ Ⓕ Ⓖ Ⓐ Ⓖ
What I'm going to say.

Ⓐ Ⓐ Ⓐ Ⓐ Ⓖ Ⓖ Ⓖ
Christmas Eve is coming soon.

Ⓕ Ⓕ Ⓕ Ⓕ Ⓐ
Now, you dear old man,

Ⓓ Ⓓ Ⓓ Ⓓ Ⓒ Ⓒ Ⓕ
Whisper what you'll bring to me.

Ⓖ Ⓕ Ⓖ Ⓐ Ⓕ
Tell me if you can.

Amazing Grace

Ⓖ Ⓒ Ⓔ Ⓒ Ⓔ Ⓓ Ⓒ Ⓐ Ⓖ
A-ma-z-ing grace! How sweet the sound,

Ⓖ Ⓒ Ⓔ Ⓒ Ⓔ Ⓓ Ⓖ
That saved a wretch like me.

Ⓔ Ⓖ Ⓔ Ⓒ Ⓖ Ⓐ Ⓒ Ⓐ Ⓖ
I once was lost, but now a'm found,

Ⓖ Ⓒ Ⓔ Ⓒ Ⓔ Ⓓ Ⓒ
Was blind but now I see.

*For a more voiced sound, change the keys
and play this variation*

Ⓒ Ⓕ Ⓐ Ⓐ Ⓖ Ⓕ Ⓓ Ⓒ
A-ma-z-ing grace! How sweet the sound,

Ⓒ Ⓕ Ⓐ Ⓐ Ⓖ Ⓒ̧
That saved a wretch like me.

Ⓐ Ⓒ̧ Ⓐ Ⓕ Ⓒ Ⓓ Ⓕ Ⓒ
I once was lost, but now a'm found,

Ⓒ Ⓕ Ⓐ Ⓐ Ⓖ Ⓕ
Was blind but now I see.

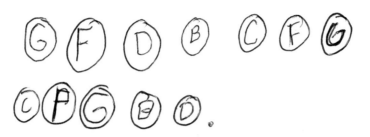

G F D B C F G
C P G B D.

Made in the
USA
Monee, IL